ENGLAND HEROES 2010

A Photos

First published by Parragon in 2010

Parragon
Queen Street House
4 Queen Street
Bath BA1 1HE, UK

Copyright © Parragon Books Ltd 2010
All information correct at time of creation, December 2009
World rankings are official FIFA figures for November 2009.
Photography © PA Photos and © Getty Images, Inc.

All rights reserved. No part of this publication may be reproduced, stored in a retrieval system or transmitted, in any form or by any means, electronic, mechanical, photocopying, recording or otherwise, without the prior permission of the copyright holder.

ISBN 978-1-4075-9499-6

Printed in China

ENGLAND HEROES 2010

Parragon

Bath · New York · Singapore · Hong Kong · Cologne · Delhi · Melbourne

ENGLAND

The Premiership is the world's most widely televised league and has nurtured a generation of talented and big match-hardened players. Combined with a favourable first-round draw, England find themselves in a relatively easy group and with a real chance for victory in South Africa. Throughout a powerful qualifying campaign, the arguments surrounding English World Cup optimism have filled the press and the airwaves.

England won the World Cup in 1966 and has maintained a consistent position as a top ten world side with a presence at every tournament since 1994. Fabio Capello is an experienced, unshakeable manager who carefully selects players from the best league in the world. The key players have immense experience and are playing at the top of their game. England's time has come, although the prospect of a penalty shoot-out is still cause for concern.

© Getty Images, Inc.

England v Croatia, World Cup Qualifier, Wembley Stadium, London, 09.09.2009

2010 WORLD CUP

EUROPE QUALIFYING FINAL GROUP 6 – FINAL TABLE

TEAM	P	W	D	L	F	A	PTS
ENGLAND	10	9	0	1	34	6	27
UKRAINE	10	6	3	1	21	6	21
CROATIA	10	6	2	2	19	13	20
BELARUS	10	4	1	5	19	14	13
KAZAKHSTAN	10	2	0	8	11	29	6
ANDORRA	10	0	0	10	3	39	0

ENGLAND PLAY	COUNTRY	DATE	VENUE
	USA	12.06.10	RUSTENBURG
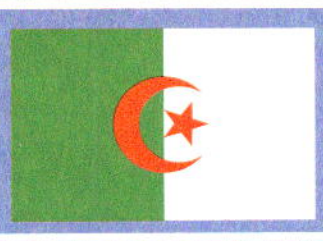	ALGERIA	18.06.10	CAPE TOWN
	SLOVENIA	23.06.10	NELSON MANDELA BAY/PORT ELIZABETH

VITAL STATISTICS

WORLD RANKING 9th
KEEPER AND DEFENCE 8/10
MIDFIELD 8/10
ATTACK 8/10

GROUP C TEAM 1

2010 World Cup

	Friday 11 June	Saturday 12 June	Sunday 13 June	Monday 14 June	Tuesday 15 June	Wednes 16 Jun
Johannesburg - JSC	South Africa - Mexico			Netherlands - Denmark		
Johannesburg - JEP		Argentina - Nigeria			Brazil - Korea DPR	
Nelspruit						Hondur - Chile
Rustenburg		England - USA			New Zealand - Slovakia	
Mangaung / Bloemfontein				Japan - Cameroon		
Cape Town	Uruguay - France			Italy - Paraguay		
Durban			Germany - Australia			Spain - Switzerla
Polokwane			Algeria - Slovenia			
Nelson Mandela Bay/ Port Elizabeth		Korea Republic - Greece			Côte d'Ivoire - Portugal	
Tshwane/ Pretoria			Serbia - Ghana			South Afr - Urugua

Group A **Group B** **Group C** **Group D**

rsday June	Friday 18 June	Saturday 19 June	Sunday 20 June	Monday 21 June	Tuesday 22 June	Wednesday 23 June	Thursday 24 June	Friday 25 June
entina - orea ublic			Brazil - Côte d'Ivoire			Ghana - Germany		
	Slovenia - USA			Spain - Honduras			Slovakia - Italy	
			Italy - New Zealand			Australia - Serbia		Korea DPR - Côte d'Ivoire
		Ghana - Australia			Mexico - Uruguay		Denmark - Japan	
eece - geria			Slovakia - Paraguay		France - South Africa			Switzerland - Honduras
	England - Algeria			Portugal - Korea DPR			Cameroon - Netherlands	
		Netherlands - Japan			Nigeria - Korea Republic			Portugal - Brazil
ance - exico					Greece - Argentina		Paraguay - New Zealand	
	Germany - Serbia			Chile - Switzerland		Slovenia - England		
		Cameroon - Denmark				USA - Algeria		Chile - Spain

Group E **Group F** **Group G** **Group H**

WORLD CUP 2010

ROUND OF 16

27 June - Johannesburg (JSC)

27 June - Bloemfontein

29 June - Pretoria

29 June - Cape Town

26 June - Port Elizabeth

26 June - Rustenburg

28 June - Durban

28 June - Johannesburg (JEP)

QUARTER-FINALS

3 July - Cape Town

3 July - Johannesburg

2 July - Johannesburg

2 July - Port Elizabeth

SEMI-FINALS

7 July - Durban

6 July - Cape Town

FINAL

11 July - Johannesburg

THIRD PLACE

10 July - Port Elizabeth

BOBBY MOORE

FACT FILE

POSITION Defender
WORLD CUP CAPS 14
GOALS 0
WINS 8
DRAWS 2
LOSSES 4
WORLD CUP HONOURS
Winner 1966

Voted England's greatest ever footballer with over half the total votes, Bobby Moore earned 108 England caps, and captained a record 90 matches. Alongside these distinctions he also won the World Cup, the FA Cup, the European Cup Winners' Cup, and was Footballer of the Year in 1964.

Moore made his England debut in an international friendly 4-0 win against Peru in May 1962, and impressed then manager Walter Winterbottom so much he stayed in the team for the duration of the World Cup in Chile. By the time England crashed out to eventual tournament winners Brazil in the Quarter-finals, Moore was noted as one to watch.

The following year a 22-year-old Moore became the youngest ever England captain in what was only his12th national appearance.

Already well established as England captain by the time Alf Ramsey took over as manager, Moore was central to the new tactical formation favoured by Ramsey – the 'wingless wonders'.

In the 1966 World Cup Final, England faced West Germany at Wembley Stadium and the stage was set for one of the greatest matches ever played. Tireless efforts and last-gasp goals meant that in extra-time, the score was 3-2 to England. While his teammates were focused on lasting out the whistle, Moore calmly set up Geoff Hurst who made it 4-2 in the dying seconds of the game and Moore led the team to collect the trophy from Queen Elizabeth II.

© PA Photos

BOBBY CHARLTON

FACT FILE

POSITION Midfielder
WORLD CUP CAPS 14
GOALS 4
WINS 8
DRAWS 2
LOSSES 4
WORLD CUP HONOURS
Winner 1966

Legendary midfielder Sir Bobby Charlton was the lynchpin of Alf Ramsey's 1966 World Cup-winning team as well as an inspirational role-model who survived the horror of the 1958 Munich air disaster which tragically claimed the lives of a number of team-mates from Manchester United.

A rare ability to play with either foot and a reputation for tireless energy during matches saw Charlton become a regular feature in England internationals during the 1960s, and he scored hat-tricks against the USA in 1959, and Mexico just two years later.

By the time he scored against Argentina in the 1962 World Cup Finals, Charlton had found the net 25 times in 38 appearances for England, and still holds the record for most goals scored at an impressive 49.

A skilful and powerful presence on the pitch, Charlton's reputation for long-range shots grew rapidly, and one such shot still holds a place as one of the most famous goals in Three Lions history. During the opener of the World Cup match against Mexico in 1966 he fired a shot into the top corner of the Mexico net from 25 yards away, typical modesty leading him to proclaim "I didn't really expect them to allow me to keep going... so I just banged it."

However, it was the two goals scored in the Semi-final against Portugal that cemented Charlton's international credentials, and although he failed to score during the Final against West Germany, there is no doubt that his persistence in attack was a major factor in the victory.

PA Photos

WORLD CUP 1966

FACT FILE

THE OCCASION World Cup Final, Wembley, 30 July 1966
WHO'S PLAYING England v West Germany
SCORE England 4, West Germany 2

Germany started off as slight favourites, so it was no surprise when they took the lead after just 12 minutes. But England were soon back in it, with Geoff Hurst heading home a free-kick from the England skipper Bobby Moore. And it stayed at 1-1 until 12 minutes from the end.

Martin Peters then put England back into the lead, tapping home from close range. The Wembley crowd went mad but then disaster struck. Germany won a free-kick, the ball cannoned off the wall and fell to the German defender Wolfgang Weber, who slotted it past the England keeper Gordon Banks to make it 2-1 to Germany.

When it came to extra time it all became very controversial. A shot by Hurst hit the underside of the bar and bounced down. "But did it cross the goal line?", the referee asked the linesman. They had a brief chat and then the referee pointed towards the centre circle. Goal! England were 3-2 up.

This time, the Germans failed to come back. With the last kick of the game, Hurst scored again and became the first player to score a hat-trick in a World Cup Final. England were World Champions.

England's captain Bobby Moore, carr shoulder high by his team-mates, holds a the FIFA World Cup, July 30, 1966. Engl defeated West Germany 4-2 in the Fi played at London's Wembley Stadi

© PA Pho

2010 FABIO CAPELLO

FACT FILE

MANAGED 21
WON 15
LOST 4
DRAWS 2
GOALS 53
GOALS CONCEDED 15

Fabio Capello is a winner. He has won a major league championship in seven of his 16 seasons as a coach and claimed domestic league titles with every club he has managed: AC Milan, Real Madrid, Roma and Juventus.

Capello is no easy-going Italian. He maintains a distance from his players and he shocked the English squad when he banned mobile phones at mealtimes. However, the team immediately responded to a man who is an astute tactician as well as an unsmiling disciplinarian. There is much for everybody to smile about with a string of well-organized victories to justify the £6 million annual salary Capello has earned since taking up the England job early in 2008.

Marcello Lippi, the manager of Italy and Capello's old friend and rival, got it about right when he spoke of Capello's appointment as England manager: 'Fabio is the type of man whose personality and charisma can bring the team together and make them all participate at the same time. He is very well prepared from a tactical point of view.'

© PA Pho

RIO FERDINAND

FACT FILE

NAME Rio Ferdinand
POSITION Defender
CAPS 76
GOALS 3
CLUB Manchester United
DATE OF BIRTH 07.11.1978
HEIGHT 188 cm
WEIGHT 77 kg
PREVIOUS CLUBS Leeds United, Bournemouth (on loan) West Ham United
INTERNATIONAL DEBUT 15.11.1997 v Cameroon
PREVIOUS WORLD CUPS 2002, 2006

Rio Ferdinand played in the 2002 and 2006 World Cups and his experience at every level of the game is underpinned with a blend of composure and speed. It's no surprise that he has been one of the first names on the England team sheet for the best part of a decade.

When needs must, Ferdinand is a traditional stopper who will give strikers a tough time, then fire the ball upfield to clear his lines. However, his more cultured technique is what distinguishes him and his ability to make the telling pass helps England play the international game of building from the back. He will also pop up in the box at set pieces to knock in the odd goal as he did in the World Cup qualifying game against Kazakhstan.

Ferdinand was barely 19 when he got his first full England cap as a substitute in a friendly against Cameroon in 1997. He developed at West Ham and Leeds and joined Manchester United in July 2002 where he has helped his club to five Premiership firsts and one Champions League title.

South Africa is probably the last chance for Ferdinand to cement his reputation as the world's best, and he will be aiming to make 11 July 2010 the day when Rio Ferdinand adds an England World Cup winners' medal to the hatful of league and cup medals he has already earned.

STYLE GUIDE

Tactically astute and, injury permitting, athletically mobile, Rio Ferdinand is the complete modern centre-back. Team awareness reinforces his attributes and he forms outstanding partnerships with the likes of Nemanja Vidić for Manchester United. The current pairing of Ferdinand with Terry makes this England central defence a rock on which most attacks will founder.

RIO FERDINAND 2010

2010 FRANK LAMPARD

Frank Lampard's service record reveals a midfield strategist who, from commanding positions at the centre of the park, plays an elegant, unruffled game creating the time and space to initiate attacks. His goal scoring is an added extra, but was something that was always expected from the man who stepped into the England side as Paul Scholes' successor.

At Chelsea, Lampard is the local hero who has fired more goals for his club than any other midfielder. Internationally he started well, scoring nine for the England under-21s, a tally only exceeded by Alan Shearer and Francis Jeffers. He got three goals in four matches as England made it to the Quarter-finals at Euro 2004, and fans voted him England Player of the Year in 2004 and 2005.

Then despite playing every minute of England's 2006 World Cup campaign, and shooting more frequently than any other England player, Lampard failed to score, and he took some of the blame when England failed to progress past the last eight.

When Fabio Capello took over the England managership in 2008, Lampard found himself playing international catch-up. He responded slowly but surely with his first international goal in two years in a 4–0 win over Slovakia in March 2009. Equally important was the assist for a Wayne Rooney goal. Now that Lampard is matching his international showings with those for Chelsea, the big question is how well he and Steven Gerrard can play in the World Cup?

STYLE GUIDE

Consistent and superbly fit, Frank Lampard is a goal-scoring midfielder with an accurate pass and a well-timed tackle. Despite the benefits of deploying him as an advanced attacking midfielder, managers like to exploit his stamina and usually instruct him to work as a box-to-box midfielder.

FRANK LAMPARD

© Getty Images, Inc.

FACT FILE

NAME Frank Lampard
POSITION Midfielder
CAPS 76
GOALS 20
CLUB Chelsea
DATE OF BIRTH 20.06.1978
HEIGHT 183 cm
WEIGHT 88 kg
PREVIOUS CLUBS West Ham United, Swansea City (loan)
INTERNATIONAL DEBUT 10.10.1999 v Belgium
PREVIOUS WORLD CUPS 2006

JOHN TERRY

FACT FILE

NAME John George Terry
POSITION Defender
CAPS 58
GOALS 6
CLUB Chelsea
DATE OF BIRTH 07.12.1980
HEIGHT 184 cm
WEIGHT 88 kg
PREVIOUS CLUBS None
INTERNATIONAL DEBUT
03.06.2003 v Serbia and Montenegro
PREVIOUS WORLD CUPS 2006

© Getty Images, Inc.

John Terry is considered one of the best centre-backs in world football and brings massive experience to Capello's England team.

Terry is an inspirational and highly effective centre-back. He was made Chelsea captain at 23, having served an apprenticeship in defensive arts when playing alongside the French World Cup-winning pair of Marcel Desailly and Frank Leboeuf. He led Chelsea to two Premier League titles in 2004–05 with the most clean sheets and the best defensive record in league history. That season he scored eight goals, including a late winner against Barcelona in the Champions League.

He made his full international debut in a friendly against Croatia in 2003. England won the game 3–1 and his main defensive partner in the victory was Rio Ferdinand. It was the beginning of an enduring international partnership that makes the English defence one of the most feared in the world. With these two players in their prime, and with both anticipating South Africa 2010 as their last chance of an England Final, opportunity and motivation could not be higher.

STYLE GUIDE

Faultless is the word that often crops up in reports of matches in which John Terry has taken a part. He is a rugged centre-back whose influence extends beyond his powerful tackle, his heading ability, his understanding of the game and his upfield forays for free kicks and corners, encouraging and commanding through force of example.

JOHN TERRY 2010

There are few better sights in football than Steven Gerrard marshalling an attack and mixing astute prodded passes with raking cross-fielders. And all the while is the exciting possibility that he'll find the net himself, as he showed at the last World Cup when he was England's top scorer.

Gerrard is a one-club man who has played in just about every position for Liverpool and scored in four major Finals, something no other English player has done. He will make himself a national hero if he can do for England what he has done for his home town.

Especially worth noting is the way he led Liverpool's comeback against AC Milan in the 2005 Champions League Final. During a six-minute stretch in the second half, Liverpool clawed back a three-goal deficit to draw 3–3 after extra-time, with Gerrard scoring one of the goals. Liverpool's third goal was from a penalty after Gerrard was brought down in Milan's penalty box. The pressing question for England fans is can Steven Gerrard push forward to repeat this in South Africa?

The Lampard/Gerrard question is key and the pair need to prove they can mesh their centrally based forward-looking skills. That said, Gerrard is a big-game player with plenty of solid international experience, not least his impressive contributions during England's serene progress through the World Cup qualifying rounds.

STYLE GUIDE

Steven Gerrard has the will and the energy to drive a team to victory and the power and pace to go with a never-say-die attitude. He is versatile and most often used in central midfield, though he can drift right or left, or move up the pitch as an auxiliary striker. He needs a free role to play at his inspirational peak.

STEVEN GERRARD 2010

STEVEN GERRARD

FACT FILE

NAME Steven Gerrard
POSITION Midfielder
CAPS 77
GOALS 16
CLUB Liverpool
DATE OF BIRTH 30.03.1980
HEIGHT 183 cm
WEIGHT 78 kg
PREVIOUS CLUBS None
INTERNATIONAL DEBUT
30.05.2000 v Ukraine
PREVIOUS WORLD CUPS 2006

PA Photos

WAYNE ROONEY

FACT FILE

NAME Wayne Rooney
POSITION Striker
CAPS 58
GOALS 25
CLUB Manchester United
DATE OF BIRTH 24.10.1985
HEIGHT 178 cm
WEIGHT 83 kg
PREVIOUS CLUB Everton
INTERNATIONAL DEBUT 12.02.2003 v Australia
PREVIOUS WORLD CUPS 2006

© Getty Images, Inc.

The hopes of a nation rest on Wayne Rooney's muscular young shoulders. He is the undisputed English footballer of his generation and with Rooney on form, England is a serious contender for World Cup glory.

Rooney's strength and balance achieve an odd grace and his sheer physicality animates teammates and crowds alike. His exciting talent and extraordinary energy have illuminated so many big games, it's hard to credit that he's not yet 25. Despite relentless press exposure and unremitting pressures of expectation, Rooney's will to win seems as fresh as when he made his England debut against Australia in 2003 and then quickly emerged as the star of Euro 2004.

An injured foot marred Rooney's (and England's) chances of significant World Cup progress in 2006. Four years ago, the nation became experts on broken metatarsals while Rooney struggled for fitness. Rooney was on less-than-peak form as England laboured towards a Quarter-final confrontation with Portugal where he was sent off after a controversial confrontation with Cristiano Ronaldo. England eventually went out on penalties.

An older, wiser Rooney will be looking to redeem himself in South Africa. With three Premier League titles and the 2008 Champions League among his club honours, he is already an Old Trafford legend where he wears the number 10 shirt. For England he is the same number, and it is likely that in South Africa he will stay up front in the spearhead role and go flat out to score.

STYLE GUIDE

Rooney rides tackles bravely to terrify defences with rollicking runs into shooting positions. The passing and the movement are clever too. His control at speed is phenomenal, he has the wit to pull off the trickiest of lobs and the power to volley with either foot.

WAYNE ROONEY

GARETH BARRY

FACT FILE

NAME Gareth Barry
POSITION Midfielder
CAPS 35
GOALS 2
CLUB Manchester City
DATE OF BIRTH 23.02.81
HEIGHT 183 cm
WEIGHT 79 kg
PREVIOUS CLUB Aston Villa
INTERNATIONAL DEBUT
31.05.00 v Ukraine
PREVIOUS WORLD CUPS None

Gareth Barry has the rare privilege of having played under five different England managers, and having won his first cap in 2000 he has been playing for England intermittently ever since.

In midfield, he forms a solid working partnership with fellow defender Steven Gerrard, but having fallen from favour during Sven-Göran Eriksson's time at the helm, Barry didn't make a single appearance for four years. It was Steve McClaren who offered Barry the second chance he needed, and he joined the team that faced, and eventually lost to, Spain at Old Trafford in February 2007.

His performance later that year during the November 2007 England v Estonia Qualifer for Euro 2008 saw him awarded Man of the Match for his part in the 3-0 England victory.

On top of this, Barry also takes full advantage of the opportunity to score goals, and has scored against Trinidad & Tobago, and in an early World Cup Qualifier against Kazakhstan in June 2009 heading a cross from Steven Gerrard to find the back of the net.

STYLE GUIDE

Barry's strong team-ethic and unselfish style provide a strong back-up for Lampard and Gerrard in midfield, as well as being able to weigh in with the odd goal.

© PA Photos

MATTHEW UPSON

Matthew Upson was signed by Arsenal after just one appearance for his first club Luton Town. After making 56 appearances for the Gunners and winning a Premier League winners' medal, Upson joined Birmingham in January 2003 before joining current club West Ham United in January 2007.

Upson's impressive performances with previous club Birmingham City led to his first international call-up in May 2003 to face South Africa.

In February 2008, Fabio Capello called on Upson to once more play for the Three Lions in a friendly against Switzerland. A powerful partnership with Rio Ferdinand helped him to firmly establish his place at the heart of England's defence. He went on to feature in the last four internationals of that year.

Amongst this was his opportunity to replace an injured John Terry for the full 90 minutes during the World Cup Qualifier against Kazakhstan in October 2008.

Upson scored his first goal for England in November 2008 in a 2-1 victory over Germany in Berlin.

FACT FILE

NAME Matthew Upson
POSITION Defender
CAPS 18
GOALS 1
CLUB West Ham United
DATE OF BIRTH 18.04.79
HEIGHT 185 cm
WEIGHT 72 kg
PREVIOUS CLUBS INCLUDE
Birmingham City, Arsenal, Lutor Town
INTERNATIONAL DEBUT
22.05.03 v South Africa
PREVIOUS WORLD CUPS None

STYLE GUIDE

Guided by Fabio Capello and West Ham boss, Gianfranco Zola, Upson's confidence has soared. Now that he is enjoying more starts, the practice of facing the best players in the world has made Upson raise his game to match, and there's every chance he will play a big role in South Africa.

© PA Photos

THEO WALCOTT

Theo Walcott became England's youngest player aged 17 years 75 days in a 3–1 defeat of Hungary. By then, Sven-Göran Eriksson had included him in the 2006 World Cup squad as back-up to Wayne Rooney and Michael Owen. The choice was controversial but the teenage prodigy came good for Fabio Capello when, in 2008, he became the youngest England hat-trick scorer in the 4–1 win over Croatia in Zagreb.

FACT FILE

NAME Theo Walcott
POSITION Striker
CAPS 8
GOALS 3
CLUB Arsenal
DATE OF BIRTH 16.03.1989
HEIGHT 175 cm
WEIGHT 68 kg
PREVIOUS CLUB Southampton
INTERNATIONAL DEBUT 30.05.2006 v Hungary
PREVIOUS WORLD CUPS 2006

At 15, he was Southampton's youngest ever reserve. He set another Southampton record when he joined the first team aged 16 years and 143 days. At the beginning of 2006, he went to Arsenal and the following August he made his Premiership debut in the first game at the new Emirates Stadium.

Walcott's status as national treasure elect was confirmed when he paraded around London carrying the Olympic flame for Beijing 2008. That parade would be as nothing compared to a 2010 World Cup victory cavalcade.

STYLE GUIDE

Walcott's blistering pace scares the defenders he runs at. When he cuts in from the right, goalkeepers quake in anticipation of powerful shots that leave them confused because they're delivered with so little backlift. If he goes to the byline, central defenders have grown wary of Walcott's accuracy with a cross.

© PA Photos

PETER CROUCH

Scoring 17 goals in the 2004-05 season for previous club side Southampton, Peter Crouch earned a call-up for the USA Tour in May 2005.

He took his place in the England side in time for a pre-World Cup friendly against Hungary in May 2006, and scored the third goal of what became a 3-0 win.

Once again showing how deadly his skills and ability to exploit a weak defence can be, Crouch donned the Three Lions in another pre-World Cup friendly, this time against Jamaica. His hat-trick of goals helped England on to the final score of 6-0.

In 2008, Crouch switched clubs from Liverpool to FA Cup winners Portsmouth, and his performance in Euro 2008 Qualifiers made him the first England player to have scored 10 goals in a single calendar year.

During qualification for South Africa, Crouch once again shone. His first-half goal against Belarus in the final Qualifier was followed up with a second goal in the 74th minute giving him 18 goals in just 17 starts.

FACT FILE

NAME Peter Crouch
POSITION Striker
CAPS 36
GOALS 18
CLUB Tottenham Hotspur
DATE OF BIRTH 30.01.81
HEIGHT 201 cm
WEIGHT 84 kg
PREVIOUS CLUBS INCLUDE Portsmouth, Liverpool, Southampton
INTERNATIONAL DEBUT 31.05.05 v Colombia
PREVIOUS WORLD CUPS 2006

© PA Photos

STYLE GUIDE

While he could form a partnership with other strikers, feeding balls to his strike partner, Crouch is a confident goalscorer in his own right and goes into every game believing he can score.

ASHLEY COLE

In 2000 the young Ashley Cole pushed aside the Brazilian international Sylvinho to claim an Arsenal place. After a mere 19 Premiership appearances, he made his international debut in a World Cup Qualifier against Albania. That year he also won his first FA Cup Final medal, something he went on to win a record five times. In 2003, he was a vital component of the Arsenal defence that lasted a whole Premiership campaign without losing a match.

His selected highlights include a few goals as well, such as the one in 2003 against Dynamo Kiev that kept Arsenal in the Champions League, and the penalty shoot-out goal that secured a 2005 FA Cup medal against Manchester United.

Sven-Göran Eriksson played Cole in a win against Albania that helped take England through to Korea/Japan 2002. Cole played in every England game in the 2006 World Cup, then continued as a first choice on the team sheets during Steve McClaren's brief reign. His form and fitness have been maintained and he'll be a key figure in Fabio Capello's plans for South Africa 2010.

FACT FILE

NAME Ashley Cole
POSITION Defender
CAPS 77
GOALS 0
CLUB Chelsea
DATE OF BIRTH 20.12.1980
HEIGHT 173 cm
WEIGHT 67 kg
PREVIOUS CLUB Arsenal
INTERNATIONAL DEBUT 28.03.2001 v Albania
PREVIOUS WORLD CUPS 2002, 2006

STYLE GUIDE

Consistent in the tackle and astute in positioning, Cole is the ultimate in efficient left-sided defenders.

© Getty Images, Inc.

DAVID JAMES

On 7 February 2008, David James was picked for Fabio Capello's first match in charge and played his first full game in England's goal since 2005 – he kept a clean sheet. What might have impressed Capello was the way James consulted sports psychologists to give him the edge at penalty kicks. These things can make all the difference.

James's stop-start international career began with a friendly against Mexico in 1997. After David Seaman's final international in 2002, James became England's first choice. He played throughout Euro 2004 but was dropped later that year following an error in a 2–2 World Cup Qualifier against Austria.

His lowest point came a year later as halftime substitute when he conceded all the goals in Denmark's 4–1 thrashing of England. But he has made more Premier League appearances than any other footballer, and has the most clean sheets in Premiership history. A couple of clean sheets could clinch it for England in South Africa and top off a distinguished career.

STYLE GUIDE

Athleticism and timing makes David James unsurpassed as a shot-stopper. However, he is also known for rushing out of the goal when he should stay put. A recent spate of injuries and long recovery time between matches have all been of concern lately.

FACT FILE

NAME David James
POSITION Goalkeeper
CAPS 49
GOALS 0
CLUB Portsmouth
DATE OF BIRTH 01.08.1970
HEIGHT 195 cm
WEIGHT 98 kg
PREVIOUS CLUBS INCLUDE Manchester City, West Ham United, Aston Villa, Liverpool, Watford
INTERNATIONAL DEBUT 29.03.1997 v Mexico
PREVIOUS WORLD CUPS 2002, 2006

© Getty Images, Inc.

ENGLAND HEROES 2010

B

BARRY, GARETH 26

C

CAPELLO, FABIO 4, 14, 17, 18, 27, 28, 29, 31
CHARLTON, BOBBY 11
COLE, ASHLEY 30
CROUCH, PETER 29

F

FERDINAND, RIO 17, 20, 21, 27

G

GERRARD, STEVEN 18, 22, 23, 26

J

JAMES, DAVID 31

L

LAMPARD, FRANK 18, 19, 22, 26

M

MOORE, BOBBY 10, 12, 13

R

RAMSEY, ALF 10, 11
ROONEY, WAYNE 18, 24, 25, 28

T

TERRY, JOHN 16, 17, 21, 27

U

UPSON, MATTHEW 27

W

WALCOTT, THEO 28
WEMBLEY STADIUM 4, 10, 12, 13
WORLD CUP FINAL 1966 4, 12, 10, 11

Page 04
TRIPLE H VS. KING BOOKER

Page 16
ROYAL

Page 26
UMAGA VS. CARLITO VS. KENNEDY

Page 36
CENA VS. ORTON

TRIPLE H VS. KING BOOKER

The showdown between King Booker and Triple H at *SummerSlam* was about more than a crown. It was about two potential future WWE Hall of Famers whose legendary careers have led to this point and feel like they have something to prove.

For weeks, the mere suggestion that there could be another king in WWE had whipped King Booker into a royal rage. Jerry "The King" Lawler's 30-year-claim to the throne threw Booker in to a rampage. But no other "blasphemous" claim had enraged the former World Heavyweight Champion more than the notion that Triple H is the "King of Kings." King Booker could not control his outrage when Lawler informed him of his *SummerSlam* match during his coronation ceremony on *Raw*. Booker gave Lawler a savage beating and clearly sent Triple H a message.

SummerSlam would mark the much-anticipated return of Triple H, who had been sidelined since *New Year's Revolution* with a quadriceps injury. The term "King of Kings" is not just a moniker for Triple H. He has won and done it all in WWE. He has had classic matches with a Who's Who of all-time greats. Triple H loves to compete – and win – on the grandest stages in sports-entertainment.

Make no mistake about it: King Booker may want this victory as badly as Triple H. Like Triple H, he has had a Hall of Fame career. But he is offended that experts so willingly refer to his opponent as the "King of Kings" yet see his monarchy as a punchline. Defeating Triple H at *SummerSlam* would put an exclamation point on King Booker's career.

"Well, King, here comes King Booker, getting ready to prove once and for all who the real King of *Raw* is!"
"Well, we all know that there is only one King of WWE, and that is me. But as for the King of *Raw*? Well, after King Booker cheap-shotted me last week, I hope that Triple H destroys him tonight and proves that really he is just a court jester!"
"Well, I guess we know who you are rooting for tonight, King, and I can't really blame you! That said, King Booker looks supremely confident coming into this match."
"Since winning the King Of The Ring tournament last year, King Booker has been looking down his nose at everybody on the roster. And tonight, he is going to be put in his place."
"Check it, J.R! He's back!"
"After nine months out of action due to injury, 'The Game' has returned!"

"And just look at him, J.R.! He looks in incredible shape!"
"It certainly looks like he has been hitting the gym pretty hard in his time away from the ring!"
"Triple H looks like he can't wait to step back into the ring tonight!"
"And I, for one, can't wait to see him back in action!"

"The crowd here at *SummerSlam* is simply going crazy for the return of Triple H!"
"I can't remember a time I have heard a reaction like this for any WWE Superstar . . . apart from me, of course!"

"Well, of course King, we all know what kind of reaction you get from the WWE fans."
"Especially those of the female variety, J.R. Speaking of which, I think I may have seen the next, ex-Mrs. Lawler in the crowd tonight!"

"King, behave yourself. The last thing you need is another wife!"
"Who said anything about getting married, J.R.?"

"Triple H sure does look impressive tonight, King!"
"Triple H has been a dominant force in WWE ever since his debut."

"He has held just about every title there is in WWE!"
"He has a championship title list longer than Joan Collins' list of boyfriends!"

"The match is underway, and Triple H immediately takes King Booker to the outside!"
"Any thoughts that King Booker may have had about Triple H suffering from a little ring rust have been knocked straight out of his head there, J.R."
"Queen Sharmell sure doesn't look too happy right now!"
"The action returns to the ring and King Booker delivers a huge chop to Triple H."
"You could hear that chop way back in the nose bleed seats, J.R.!"

"It didn't seem to have much of an effect on Triple H though. He is back in control with a Figure-Four Leglock."
"But Booker makes it to the ropes!"
"And from out of nowhere, King Booker hits Triple H with a huge superkick!"
"Both men are down, J.R.! The referee has started the 10 count!"
"Triple H is back to his feet first and catches King Booker with a stiff right hand to the jaw!"
"King Booker is looking a little wobbly after that shot, J.R.!"

"Triple H follows up with a devastating clothesline which sends King Booker down to the mat!"
"Triple H nearly took King Booker's head clean off with that move, J.R.!"
"Triple H is on fire here tonight!"
"You're right, King! Triple H looks as solid as ever!"
"Wait a second, J.R. We shouldn't count King Booker out just yet!"
"The Bookend! King Booker just hit the Bookend on Triple H and is going for the pin! One... two... Triple H kicks out at two!"

"Queen Sharmell can't believe it! She thought her man had the match in the bag right there!"
"King Booker has gone to the top rope here, King!"
"King Booker is continuing the onslaught with a huge sidewalk slam!"
"I could feel that move from here, J.R.!"
"He's going for a front flip legdrop! But Triple H moves out of the way!"
BOOKER T.

"Both men are back to their feet! And look, King! Triple H is giving King Booker the DX crotch chop!"
"He may be signalling the end for King Booker here, J.R.!"
"Triple H with a big boot to the mid-section!"
"I think we all know what is coming next J.R.!"
"PEDIGREE! Triple H hit the Pedigree on King Booker!"
"He is going for the pin! One... two... three! Triple H wins! Triple H wins!"

"What a triumphant return for Triple H!"
"He has truly proven that he is indeed, the 'King Of Kings'!"

" What is next for 'The Game,' King?"
"Who knows, J.R.? But in the form he has shown this evening, surely he will be chasing the WWE Championship somewhere down the road!"

DIVAS BATTLE ROYAL

The "Biggest Party of the Summer" wouldn't have been complete without the beautiful WWE Divas. Recognising the appeal of a scintillating showdown, *Raw* general manager William Regal conferred with his colleagues from *SmackDown* and *ECW* and arranged for a Battle Royal among all WWE Divas at *SummerSlam*. The winner of the match would get an opportunity to challenge Candice Michelle for the Women's Championship.

The Battle Royal could be a big break for newcomers like Beth Phoenix, who is anxious to make an impact in WWE, and Divas like Jillian, Michelle McCool, or the ladies of Extreme Exposé, who have not had an opportunity at the Women's Championship. The match also signified the prospect of redemption for former Women's Champions such as Melina, Victoria and Mickie James.

Who would win the Battle Royal and have a chance at taking on Women's Champion Candice Michelle? There's only one way to find out, turn the page and check it out!

"Well, King. This is the match you have been waiting for, the Divas Battle Royal!"
"You know me, J.R.! I can't get enough of the WWE Divas!"
"There you see WWE Women's Champion Candice Michelle!"
"The winner of the Battle Royal will receive a shot at Candice's title."

"All the Divas are in the ring, and the war has begun!"
"This is full-on Diva action, J.R.!"

"Kristal delivers a boot to Kelly Kelly's midsection!"
"I hope Kelly is OK, J.R.! I think I had best get in there and check!"

"You stay right where you are, King! I know the kind of first aid you want to administer!"
"What, J.R.? I was only thinking about the Divas!"

"These girls are really going at it! I have never seen anything like this!"
"I have, J.R.! Of course, I was sleeping at the time!"
"There goes Maria! She's out of the match!"
"Kelly Kelly is doing so well considering this is her first Battle Royal!"
"Kelly Kelly, so hot they named her twice!"
"Beth Phoenix could be following her pretty soon!"

"Phoenix manages to hold on. Now Melina has found herself in a tricky predicament in the corner!"
"Phoenix is just so strong, J.R."
"Kristal is about to be eliminated!"
"Not Kristal, she is one of my favourites, J.R!"

"All the Divas are your favourite, King!"
"OK, OK, you're right! It's just so hard to pick one of these beautiful women!"
"Melina is really laying the boots in there!"
"Laying the boots in to Layla!"
"The former Women's Champion really does have a mean streak!"
"Melina really is a deliciously devious Diva, J.R.!"

"Nice alliteration there, King!"
"Thanks, partner. But what is alliteration?"
"It is meant to be every Diva for themselves, but these two seem to be teaming up here, King!"
"That won't last for long, J.R.! I can guarantee that!"
"Beth Phoenix may be on her way out here, King!"
"She has a vise-like grip on those ropes though, J.R.!"

"Phoenix has managed to stay in the match and has Kelly Kelly up in the corner!"
"Phoenix could win this whole thing, J.R.!"

"Torrie Wilson and Michelle McCool take Phoenix down with a hard double clothesline!"

"They are going to have to work together if they want to take out this 'Glamazon'!"

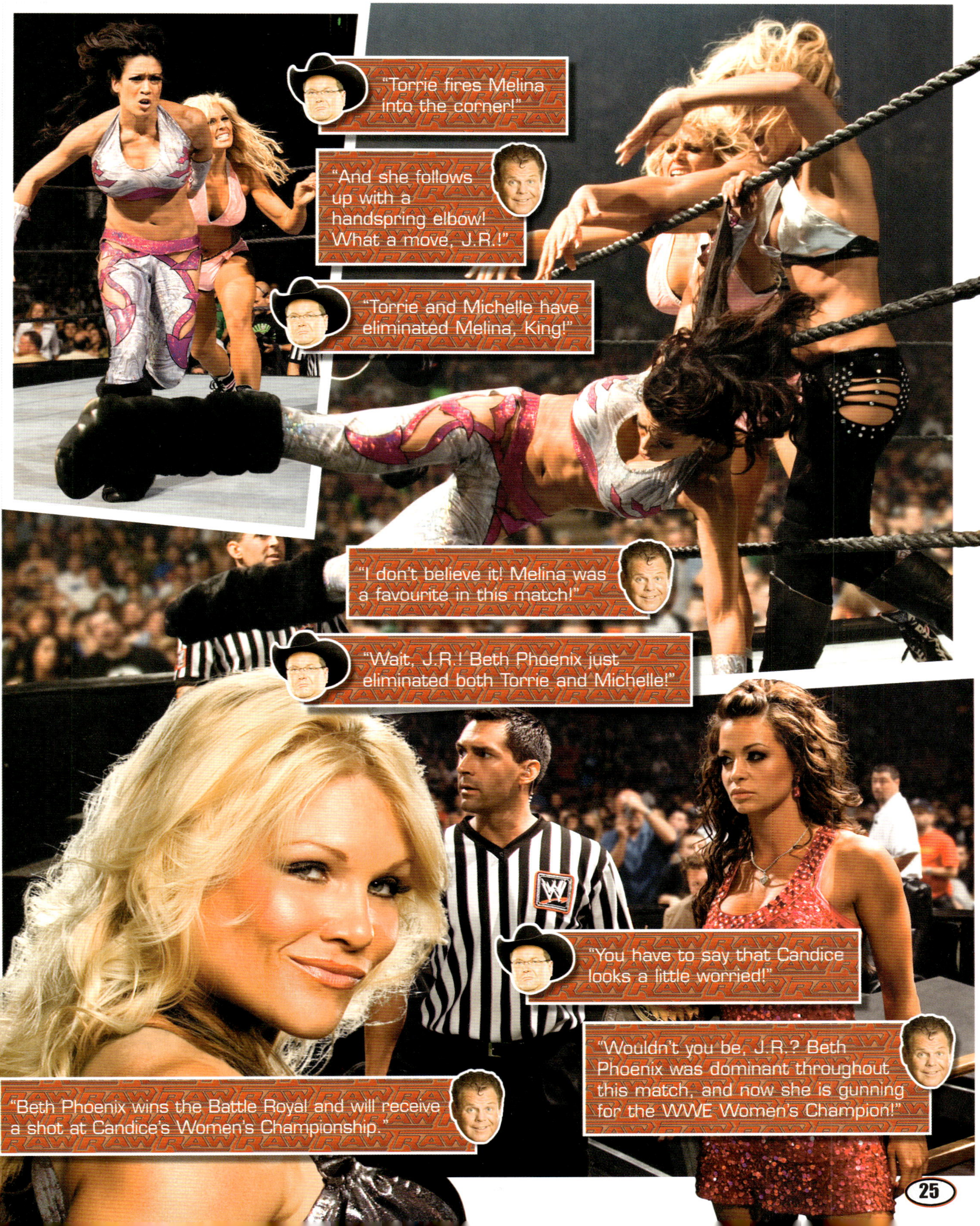
"Torrie fires Melina into the corner!"
"And she follows up with a handspring elbow! What a move, J.R.!"
"Torrie and Michelle have eliminated Melina, King!"
"I don't believe it! Melina was a favourite in this match!"
"Wait, J.R.! Beth Phoenix just eliminated both Torrie and Michelle!"
"You have to say that Candice looks a little worried!"
"Wouldn't you be, J.R.? Beth Phoenix was dominant throughout this match, and now she is gunning for the WWE Women's Champion!"
"Beth Phoenix wins the Battle Royal and will receive a shot at Candice's Women's Championship."

UMAGA
VS.
CARLITO
VS.
MR. KENNEDY

One-on-one, very few Superstars have ever been able to handle Intercontinental Champion Umaga. The "Samoan Bulldozer" seems impervious to pain at times. He knows no loyalties and knows only one speed when he brutalises his foes in the ring – full speed. And lately, in recent matches against Marella, Jeff Hardy, Carlito, Cena, and Randy Orton, he has looked unstoppable.

Still, Umaga may be facing his toughest challenge yet when he defends his Intercontinental Championship against two of WWE's hungriest Superstars at *SummerSlam*, Carlito and Mr. Kennedy. This Triple Threat Match was made on *Raw* after a Kennedy-Carlito contest to determine who would face Umaga at *SummerSlam* ended without a decisive winner. *Raw* GM William Regal decided that having a Triple Threat Match for the Intercontinental Championship would best serve the combatants and fans.

Could Umaga cement his dominant hold on the Intercontinental Championship at *SummerSlam*? Or would Kennedy and Carlito be too much even for the "Samoan Bulldozer"?

AND THERE'S THE BELL!

"Well J.R., Carlito is already in the ring. And here comes Mr. Kennedy!"
"Kennedy is one of the most gifted athletes on *Raw* right now!"
"That said, I don't know if anyone on *Raw* has the skills to stop the 'Samoan Bulldozer'!"
"Umaga has decimated his opponents since his debut in 2006."
"You are right, King. Since Umaga became part of WWE, only a precious few have defeated him!"
"And when you look at him, you can see why, J.R.!"

"There's no denying it, Umaga is a monster!"
"It seems like he just loves to hurt people, J.R."
"It looks like Kennedy is trying to convince Umaga to work with him!"
"I don't think that is going to work out, J.R.!"

"Mr. Kennedy with a big right hand to Carlito!"
"That will have loosened some teeth!"

"Kennedy is stomping a mudhole in Carlito!"
"Kennedy is really going to town with those kicks!"
"Kennedy shoots Carlito into the ropes."
"But Carlito comes back with that springboard elbow manoeuvre!"
"Mr. Kennedy retaliates with a takedown, and slams Carlito's face into the mat!"
"That had to hurt!"

"Umaga is back in the ring, and he comes off the top rope with a devastating splash!"
"Umaga is so agile for such a big man!"
"Umaga is climbing to the top again!"
"But wait, J.R.! Kennedy has picked up a television monitor from the Spanish announce table!"
"Kennedy with a thunderous shot to the head of the 'Samoan Bulldozer'!"
"Umaga must be knocked out cold!"

"Kennedy and Carlito are taking advantage of the big man being down!"
"They are hammering away on him with this double-team manoeuvre!"
"Carlito and Kennedy are going to suplex Umaga!"
"Can they get him up there?"
"I don't believe it! Umaga has reversed the suplex and taken both Kennedy and Carlito over!"
"This Umaga must be superhuman, J.R.!"

"Umaga comes off the ropes with a double clothesline that takes down both his opponents!"
"Umaga is in complete control here!"
"Umaga with a huge kick to Carlito!"
"What impact, J.R.!"
"Umaga charges at Kennedy!"
"But Kennedy's smart enough to pull down the top rope, J.R!"

"Umaga holds on, King! And he's straight back into the ring !"
"I can't see this match going much longer, J.R.!"
"You're right, King! Umaga just hit the Samoan Spike on Mr. Kennedy!"

"Umaga is going for the pin!"
"1...2...3! It's over! Umaga has retained the Intercontinental Championship!"

"Umaga leaves *SummerSlam* as he came in, Intercontinental Champion!"

"It looks like a bomb site in the ring, J.R.! Umaga was simply unstoppable tonight!"

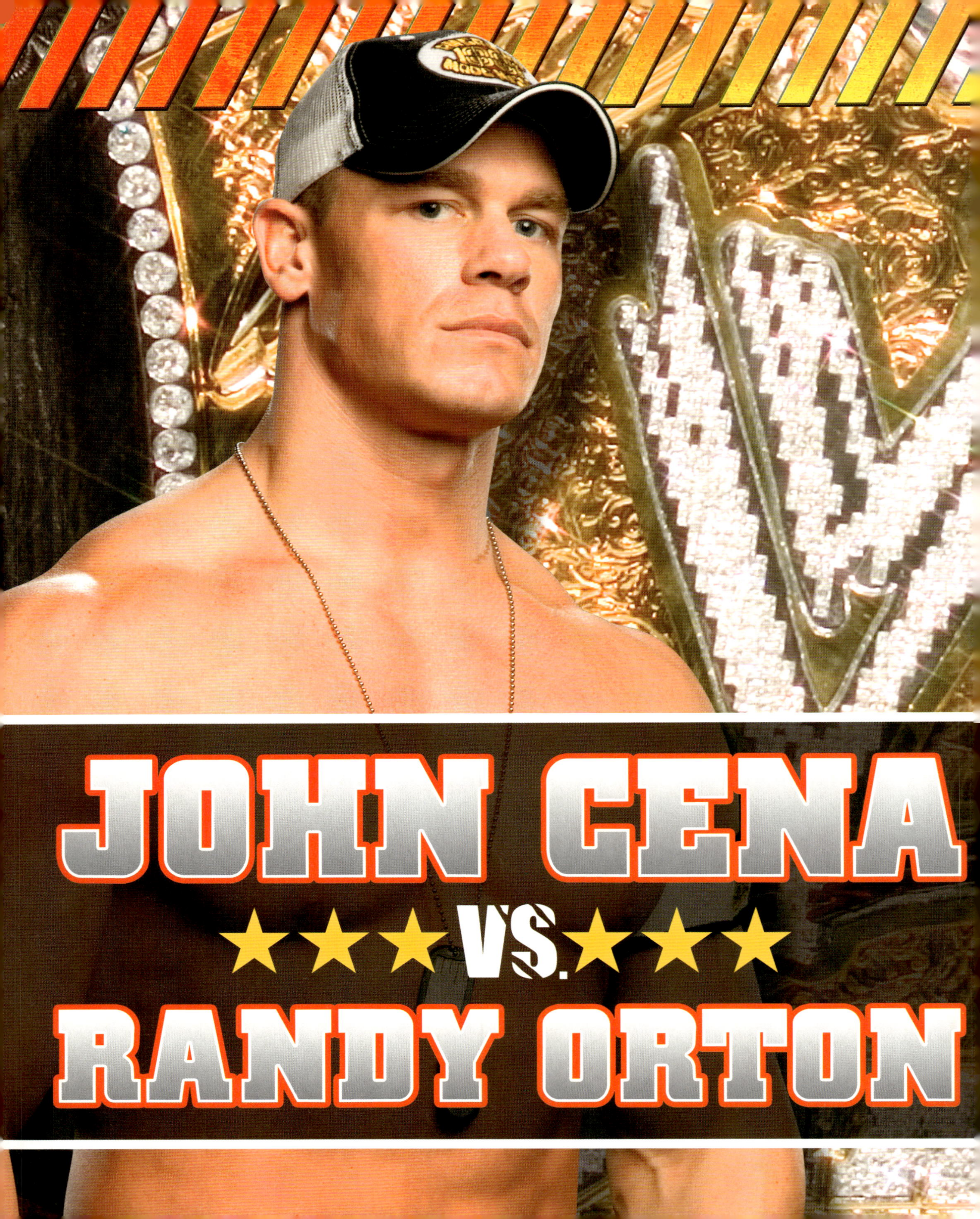

JOHN CENA VS. RANDY ORTON

Randy Orton sees the WWE Championship differently than the other Superstars. It doesn't just represent sports-entertainment's most coveted prize. To Orton, a third-generation Superstar, it represents his destiny.

As WWE Champion, Cena is a legend in the making. He has held the championship for 24 of the last 27 months and had been on an incredible roll in his third reign as champion. From Edge to Umaga, from Shawn Michaels to Bobby Lashley, he had turned back the challenges of all comers for the previous 11 months.

However, Cena had not faced Orton one-on-one with the WWE Championship on the line. The two had faced off in tag team matches and with several other competitors involved in WWE Championship matches, but they'd never battled mano-a-mano. At *SummerSlam*, Orton had the opportunity to fulfil his potential and become the champion that so many have predicted he will be.

Cena had to be careful because Orton is cold, calculating and sadistic. The WWE Champion may have been facing his most dangerous opponent. But if Cena is able to turn back Orton's challenge, he will not only extend his championship reign, but may cement his own legacy – and destiny – as one of the greatest champions in WWE history.

"Well, here comes the challenger, Randy Orton!"
"Orton has been obsessed with John Cena's title for over a year now!"
"And here comes the champ, set for what may be one of his biggest title defences of his career!"
HUSTLE LOYALTY RESPECT
"John Cena looks to be totally focused on the task at hand here tonight!"
"The match is underway, and John Cena takes Orton down with a headlock takeover."
"I really wasn't expecting this match to be this technical, J.R."

"Orton reverses it with a headlock of his own!"
"Randy Orton is such a great ring technician!"
"Cena is back in control, slamming Orton's face into the mat!"
"You're not wrong, King! It's shaping up to be a real slobberknocker!"
"The momentum in this match is so back and forth!"
"Look at this! Orton has Cena in a sleeper hold, and the champ is fading fast!"

"Orton is stomping away on the WWE Champion!"
"But here comes Cena with a head of steam! Cena takes Orton down with a huge flying shoulder tackle!"
"He is really going to town with those boots to the midsection!"
"Did you see the hang time Cena had on that move J.R.?"
"Say it with me, J.R.! YOU CAN'T SEE ME!"
"Cena looks like he may be going for the Five-Knuckle Shuffle here, King!"

"What impact from the WWE Champion, dropping that huge fist of his right into Orton's face!"
"No doubt about it, it is an impressive manoeuvre!"
"Wait! Orton is back to his feet!"
"From out of nowhere, Orton hits his modified backbreaker on the champion, and Orton is back in control!"

"Check this out J.R.! Orton has Cena set up for a DDT!"
"Orton has taken so many opponents out with this move recently. If he hits it, the match will be over!"
"Orton drives Cena face first into the mat! This should be over, King!"
"Orton should be going for the pin! What does he have in mind here?"
"I think he is looking for the RKO!"
"Cena blocks the RKO and comes off the ropes with a huge shoulder block!"
"The tide could be turning in Cena's favour!"

"Cena is ascending to the top rope!"
"But Orton is there to meet him with some big right hands!"
"Both men are on the top turnbuckle exchanging blows!"
"Cena over powers Orton and sends him crashing back down to the canvas!"

"Cena leaps from the top with a huge legdrop to the prone Randy Orton!"
"Cena is not known as a high-flyer, but you wouldn't have guessed it from that move!"

"Cena's going high-risk here!"
"But Orton moves out of the way!"

"Cena slowly makes his way back to his feet, and he's met with a spectacular dropkick from Orton!"
"Did you see the elevation that Orton got on his vertical leap? What an athlete, J.R.!"
"Out of nowhere, John Cena locks in the STFU! Orton has to escape or the match will be over!"
"Orton reaches the ropes and hits Cena with a blatant low blow while the referees back is turned!"
"Orton is stalking the champion, possibly looking for another attempt at the RKO!"
"Orton will literally do anything to win here, J.R."

"Orton goes for the RKO, but Cena reverses it and has Orton set for the F-U!"
"What an incredible reversal, but can Cena hit his signature manoeuvre?"
"F-U! F-U!"

"Cena goes for the pin! One... two... three! It's all over!"
"Cena retains the WWE Championship!"
"What a battle, King! At times it looked like Cena was out of the match, but his resilience shone through in the end!"
"I really thought Orton was going to win this, J.R.!"